ISBN: 978-1-938117-71-8
[Print Edition]

I0154990

EVERYDAY ARABIC SERIES (BOOK 2)

This book teaches the Arabic vocabulary for:

1. Objects: Fruit

2. Characteristics: Colors

3. Locations: Inside & Outside

Age Level [Basic: Ages 4-6 & Above]

Apples	*At-Tuffaah*	التُّفَّاحُ
Bananas	*Al-Mawz*	المَوَز
Blueberries	*At-Toot Al-Inabiyyah*	التُّوْتُ الْعِنَبِيَّةُ
Cherries	*Al-Karaz*	الْكَرَزُ
Coconuts	*Jawz Al-Hind*	جَوَزُ الْهِنْدُ
Raspberries	*At-Toot Ash-Shawki*	التُّوتُ الشَّوْكِي
Kiwis	*Al-Kiwi*	الكيوي
Grapefruit	*Al-Kraybfroot*	الكَرِيبْ فَرُوْتْ
Melons	*Ash-Shammaam*	الشَّمَّامُ
Oranges	*Al-Burtuqaal*	الْبُرْتُقالُ
Pomegranates	*Ar-Rummaan*	الرُّمَّانُ
Lemons	*Al-Laymoon*	اللَّيْمُونُ
Limes	*Al-Leem*	الْلِيْم
Pears	*Al-Kamthari*	الْكَمْثَرى
Plums	*Al-Khawkh*	الْخَوْخُ
Tangerines	*Al-Yusufi*	الْيُوسُفِيُّ
Watermelon	*Al-Bitteekh*	الْبِطِّيخُ
Grapes	*Al-Inab*	الْعِنَبُ
Strawberries	*Al-Farawlah*	الْفَرَاوَلَةُ

Apples are red and green outside and white inside.

التُّفَّاحُ أَحْمَرُ وَأَخْضَرُ مِنَ الْخَارِجِ وَأَبْيَضُ مِنَ الدَّاخِلِ.

Bananas are yellow outside and white inside.

المَوز أَصفَرُ مِنَ الخَارِجِ وَأَبيَضُ مِنَ الدَّاخِلِ.

Blueberries are blue outside and blue inside.

التُّوْتُ الْعِنَبِيَّةُ أَزْرَقُ مِنَ الْخَارِجِ وَأَزْرَقُ مِنَ الدَّاخِلِ.

Cherries are **red** outside and **red** inside.

الْكَرَزُ أَحْمَرُ مِنَ الْخَارِجِ وَأَحْمَرُ مِنَ الدَّاخِلِ.

Coconuts are **brown outside** and **white inside**.

جوَزُ الْهِنْدْ بُنْيٌ مِنَ الْخَارِجِ وَأَبْيَضُ مِنَ الدَّاخِلِ.

Raspberries are red outside and red inside.

التُّوت الشَّوْكي أَحْمَرُ مِنَ الْخَارِجِ وَأَحْمَرُ مِنَ الدَّاخِلِ.

Kiwis are brown outside and green inside.

الكيوي بُنِّيٌّ مِنَ الْخَارِجِ وَأَخْضَرُ مِنَ الدَّاخِلِ.

Grapefruit are yellow outside and pink inside.

الْكَرِيبْ فَرُوْث أَصْفَرُ مِنَ الْخَارِجِ وَوَرْدِي مِنَ الدَّاخِلِ.

Melons are yellow outside and white inside.

الشَّمامُ أَصْفَرُ مِنَ الْخَارِجِ وَأَبْيَضُ مِنَ الدَّاخِلِ.

Oranges are orange outside and orange inside.

الْبُرْتُقَالُ بُرْتُقَالِي مِنَ الْخَارِجِ وَبُرْتُقَالِي مِنَ الدَّاخِلِ.

Pomegranates are red outside and red inside.

الرُّمَّانُ أَحْمَرُ مِنَ الْخَارِجِ وَأَحْمَرُ مِنَ الدَّاخِلِ.

Lemons are yellow outside and yellow inside.

اللَّيْمُونُ أَصْفَرُ مِنَ الْخَارِجِ وَأَصْفَرُ مِنَ الدَّاخِلِ.

Limes are green outside and green inside.

اللِّيْمُ أَخْضَرُ مِنَ الْخَارِجِ وَأَخْضَرُ مِنَ الدَّاخِلِ.

Pears are yellow outside and white inside.

الْكَمْثَرى أَصْفَرُ مِنَ الْخَارِجِ وَأَبْيَضُ مِنَ الدَّاخِلِ.

Plums are red outside and yellow inside.

الْخَوْخُ أَحْمَرُ مِنَ الْخَارِجِ وَأَصْفَرُ مِنَ الدَّاخِلِ.

Tangerines are orange outside and orange inside.

الْيُوسُفِيُّ بُرْتُقَالِيٌّ مِنَ الْخَارِجِ وَبُرْتُقَالِيٌّ مِنَ الدَّاخِلِ.

Watermelons are green outside and red inside.

الْبِطِّيخُ أَخْضَرُ مِنَ الْخَارِجِ وَأَحْمَرُ مِنَ الدَّاخِلِ.

Grapes are **purple** or **green** **outside** and colorless **inside**.

الْعِنَبُ أَرَجَوَانِي أَوَ أَخْضَرُ مِنَ الْخَارِجِ وَبِدُوْنِ لَوْنِ مِنَ الدَّاخِلِ.

Strawberries are red outside and red inside.

الْفَرَاوِلَةُ أَحْمَرُ مِنَ الْخَارِجِ وَأَحْمَرُ مِنَ الدَّاخِلِ.

Instructions:

1. Color the picture of the biggest fruit.
2. Next color the picture of the fruit which is brown outside.
3. Next color the picture of the fruit which is yellow outside.

(Afterward you can color the rest of the fruit)

تَعْلِيمَات:

١. لَوِّنْ صُورَةُ أَكْبَرُ الْفواكه.

٢. ثُمَّ لَوِّنْ صُورَةُ الْفَاكِهَةِ الَّتِي لَوَنها بُنِّيٍّ مِنَ الْخَارِج.

٣. ثُمَّ لَوِّنْ صُورَةُ الْفَاكِهَةِ الَّتِي لَوَنها أَصْفَرُ مِنَ الْخَارِج.

(بَعْدَ ذَلِكَ يُمْكِنُكَ تَلْوِينِ بَقِيَّةِ الْفواكهَ)

Questions:

1. How many of the fruits you colored are white inside?

2. How many of the fruits you colored are red inside?

3. What is the biggest kind of fruit you colored?

الأسْئِلَةُ:

١. كَمْ عَدَدُ الْفواكهِ الَّتِي لَوَنها أَبِيَضُ مِنَ الدَّاخِلِ؟

٢. كَمْ عَدَدُ الْفواكهِ الَّتِي لَوَنها أَحْمَرُ مِنَ الدَّاخِلِ؟

٣. مَا هُوَ أَكْبَرُ نُوعٍ مِنَ الفواكهَ الَّتِي لَوَّنْتَهَا؟

Instructions:

1. Color the picture of the longest fruit.

2. Next color the picture of the fruit which is brown outside.

3. Next color the picture of the fruit which is red outside.

(Afterward you can color the rest of the fruit)

تَعْلِيمَات:

١. لَوِّنْ صُوَرَةُ أَطُولُ الْفواكهَ.

٢. ثَمَّ لَوِّنْ صُورَةِ الْفَاكِهَةِ الَّتِي لَوْنَهَا بُنْيٌّ مِنَ الْخَارِجِ.

٣. ثَمَّ لَوِّنْ صُورَةِ الْفَاكِهَةِ الَّتِي لَوْنَهَا أَحْمَرُ مِنَ الْخَارِجِ.

(بَعْدَ ذَلِكَ يُمْكِنُكَ تَلْوِيْنِ بَقِيَّةِ الْفواكهَ)

Questions:

1. How many of the fruits you colored are the same color inside and outside?
2. How many of the fruits you colored are yellow outside?
3. What is the longest kind of fruit you colored?

الأَسْئِلَةُ:

١. كَمْ عَدَدُ الْفواكه الَّتِي لَوَنها نَفْسُ اللَّوْنَ مِنَ الدَّاخِلِ وَمِنَ الْخَارِجِ؟

٢. كَمْ عَدَدُ الْفواكه الَّتِي لَوَنها أَصْفَرُ مِنَ الْخَارِج؟

٣. مَا هُوَ أَطْوَلُ نَوْعٍ مِنَ الْفواكه الْمُلَوَّنَة؟

TITLES IN THIS SERIES:

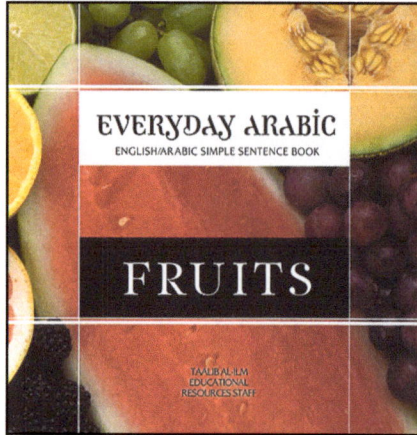

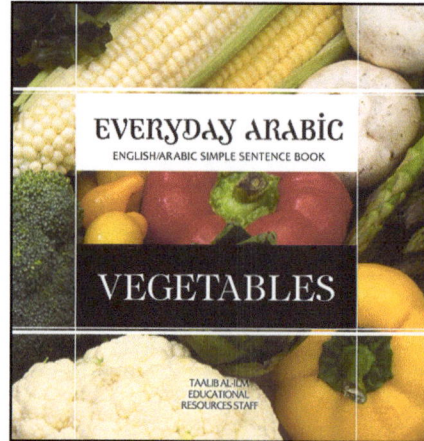

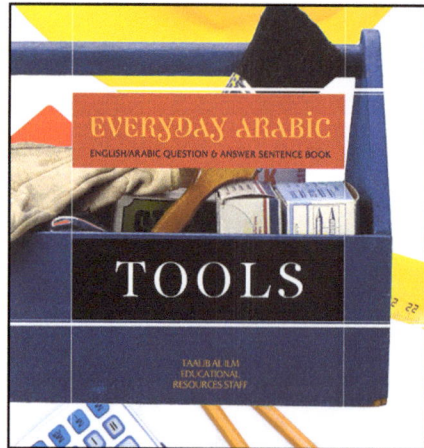

EVERYDAY ARABIC
ENGLISH/ARABIC SIMPLE SENTENCE BOOK
FRUITS
TAALIB AL-ILM
EDUCATIONAL
RESOURCES STAFF

EVERYDAY ARABIC
ENGLISH/ARABIC SIMPLE SENTENCE BOOK
VEGETABLES
TAALIB AL-ILM
EDUCATIONAL
RESOURCES STAFF

EVERYDAY ARABIC
ENGLISH/ARABIC QUESTION & ANSWER SENTENCE BOOK
KITCHEN ITEMS
TAALIB AL-ILM
EDUCATIONAL
RESOURCES STAFF

EVERYDAY ARABIC
ENGLISH/ARABIC QUESTION & ANSWER SENTENCE BOOK
TOOLS
TAALIB AL-ILM
EDUCATIONAL
RESOURCES STAFF

TITLES IN THIS SERIES:

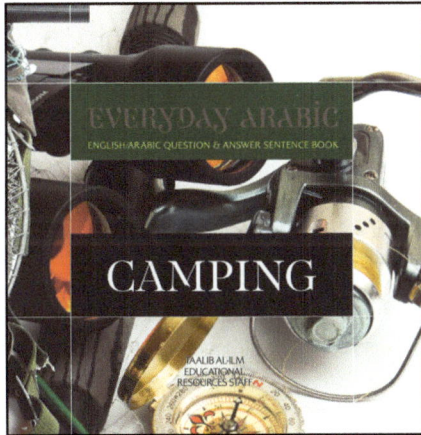

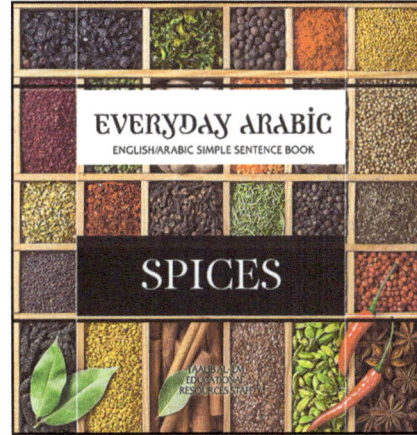

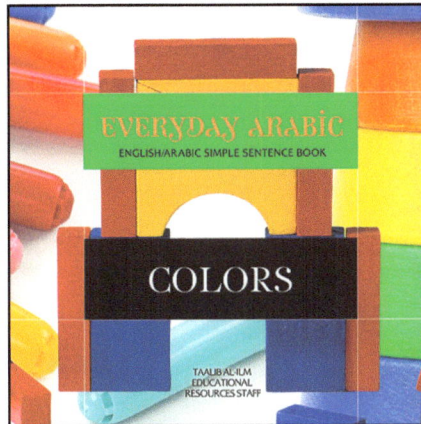

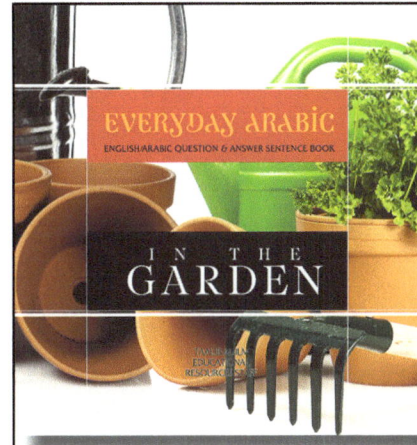

EVERYDAY ARABIC
ENGLISH/ARABIC QUESTION & ANSWER SENTENCE BOOK
CAMPING
TAALIB AL-ILM
EDUCATIONAL
RESOURCES STAFF

EVERYDAY ARABIC
ENGLISH/ARABIC SIMPLE SENTENCE BOOK
SPICES
TAALIB AL-ILM
EDUCATIONAL
RESOURCES STAFF

EVERYDAY ARABIC
ENGLISH/ARABIC SIMPLE SENTENCE BOOK
COLORS
TAALIB AL-ILM
EDUCATIONAL
RESOURCES STAFF

EVERYDAY ARABIC
ENGLISH/ARABIC QUESTION & ANSWER SENTENCE BOOK
IN THE GARDEN
TAALIB AL-ILM
EDUCATIONAL
RESOURCES STAFF

www.ingramcontent.com/pod-product-compliance
Lightning Source LLC
LaVergne TN
LVHW072125070426
835511LV00003B/86

9 781938 117718